Arrhythmia

Poems that come from the heart
by Joseph (Joe) Baer

I0530385

For

My favorite professor, for inspiring me to embrace my own writing style and create these poems to begin with!

My big sis for supporting me and being the one person I can always talk to,

and My mom who encourages me to pursue my dreams because I can accomplish anything through my efforts.

Table of Contents

Fool for U

I love you
Like driving with the windows down at night
Like winter cuddles by the firelight
Like the feeling I get inside my chest
Each time I feel your soft caress
Or warm embrace that lights my fire
And it is my feelings for you that never tire
I must admit I still have feelings
After all this time my heart kept beating
Only for you I'll keep repeating
I love you
I love you
I love you

Love Poem for a Car

5 Mississippis before the doors lock
Goodnight
Unplugged the bluetooth adapter from its socket
The white noise hushes, the volume turns low

We don't go out much to save on gas
Long trip home, costs vary, but not bad
Got my dad's lead foot, love to pass

Usually wearing my boots,
Always listening to my tunes
and you always wear the same shade of blue
You and I both do

I hope we go on many more adventures together
Maybe bring some friends along with us
Or just you, me and the open road

Collapse
(In loving memory of the AT Still University Water Tower,
Kirksville MO)

Watching each day from miles around the epicenter of the
event
Two people stood atop the monument

In front of all, for eyes to see
A crane peels the layers sliced away sheet by sheet

A painting of this tower now looks incomplete
Where the sky and clouds show through up one hundred and
thirty feet

Should hope they build another one, firstly
So that the community doesn't go thirsty

Rest assured
and don't buckle under the pressure

For however attached you become
There will always be another that comes along

After all, this tower has had a long run and also deserves rest
Through rain or shine, it has always done its best

For that it has earned our respect and will be dearly missed
Tower, rest in peace now that by death you have been kissed

Used to be, Baby

"Baby"
   "Baby"
"Baby"
   "Baby"
This went on
And continues on
In memory
An infinite thread
Weaving back and through and then back again
To the times I don't want to forget

But she wanted new names
"Beby" was the alternative
To her memory
And "Kitty" was off the table
Ex boyfriend, obviously

And I told myself over and over
That I wouldn't write another poem
But memory, in its infinite thread
Brought me back
Goddamnit

I don't miss it
Because it's still with me
She doesn't miss it
Because she's moved on
New boyfriend, obviously

And we all have a past

Heartaches and Love Letters

~

Full of mistakes that you learn from
People are left behind or move away
and maybe
You loved them
You didn't think it at first
But then you started to realize

How could you have known?
You never knew any better
Don't blame yourself
For the things that
used to be, baby
You don't have to worry
Since the past
Is in the past

You are not the same person
you were, and neither are they
I'm all go with the flow, baby
No, there's no need to worry, baby
There's always tomorrow, baby

Poem for a Stranger

I saw you first, last I can recall
Hooded, hands in pockets, hunched slightly in the cold slush
Of that empty parking lot
You heading west
Myself, eastbound
Your cheeks pink, it could have been below freezing
Call it 33 degrees
Exchanged glances
I smiled at you
Maybe you smiled too
Hard to say
I wish I was walking with you in that westerly direction
So I could get to know you
And your affection
You might be the cutest thing I've seen in months
Several, in fact
I just love your round glasses (so much)

I don't think I've ever seen you before, last I can recall
After all, it's just a little baby crush
And I think about you a lot
Daydreaming is the best
Better than a rebound
Another relationship could prove pleasing
So stranger, please
Accept my advances
The things I wouldn't do
To experience something new
To the lord, I pray
For some kind of personal connection

Heartaches and Love Letters

~

Much stronger than those few
I learn from reflection
A love that I had once
Magnets that attract
But the connection between them passes

Last I can recall, love was more than attraction
I haven't even tasted it all, all that mush
Some of it is warm, some of it's hot
Not all of it is on the test
If you swim, not float, you'll drown
It's an ocean out there full of fish, even teeming
So sailor, breathe
You'll have plenty of chances
Many boats will pass through
This dock bobbing in an ocean pool
Waiting for Saturday
To release the ropes of circumspection
That bind the things you wouldn't do
Things that change your direction
Help you find balance
Put one foot in front of the other
And soon you are walking out the door
You'll never get where you're going
If you never get up on your feet
I didn't even turn around that day
Now, Snowgirl, we'll never meet

Love Letter #19

I want to cook and bake for you, with you
I want to draw and paint you, still with you
What do you want to do and share with me?
I want to do anything with you
I want to do absolutely nothing with you
What do you ask of me?
As you wish
I wish these things and more
I wish we continue to make memories
I wish you could see me the way I see you
What do you wish?
I want that for you
Have I helped any of your wishes come true?
I sure hope so
I hope we never stop losing track of time
I hope you like that I call you mine
And you can call me yours, too
I'm your fool
Please don't fool with my heart
My heart has seen a lot
I want to see and feel yours, too
Let's trade like card games and monopoly property
What's stopping me is I don't want this game with you to end
since it isn't really a game anymore
And you should know that I would never treat you like a toy
I'm just a boy standing
Here in front of me is a good place and I want to see your
face everyday from now on
* I love you, silly *

Eyes

Eyes can kiss too
Like butterflies
Swimming in beautiful skies
Colorful
Melancholy
Distant
Fluttering away as I try to make contact
I give up, for I cannot chase them where they are going

I miss them just as much, if not more,
For fine wood, nor pools of honey could compare

No, the ones I miss are still as pure and bright as I remember
As bright as what, I cannot say

And in my dreams I do not see them
Elusive
Withholding
I wonder what they see, what they want
Or if they're looking right through me

I want to read your eyes like a book I can't put down
I want to hear everything your eyes have to say
They captivate me, I can never get enough
Don't you dare look away
Look me in the eyes
I want to see the way you feel about me
Inside those butterflies

For the Love of Kisses

~

Juliet

Your purple lip
Like a sweet flower it doth kiss
My cheeks and just above the hip
I wish not to be only just a friend
So please grant, I ask of you, my wish
"Give me my sin again"

For the Love of Kisses

I have a couple girls on my mind
But I wouldn't kiss them like I want to
Because it would remind me of how I kissed you
I haven't kissed and probably won't kiss
Even though I want to so
It pains me to have to let it go
Kissing is my favorite thing you see
But when I kiss I fall in love too easily
A kiss is more than a kiss to me
And kisses filled with meaning make my heart sing
I want to kiss you tonight
But my dear, I lose you just like before
Under the moonlight
I shed a single tear as I recall those days
I kissed her so
Goodbye, sweet and tender kiss
Your warm embrace, I will dearly miss
Please come back to me
For I yearn to be in your company

Night is Young

Kiss me
Before the night is through
Night is young
Your kiss wouldn't miss its mark
Before the dark departs
So kiss me and hold me in your heart
Before the night is through

Interlude

I never really knew why she left other than separate paths.
Why can't you stay?
Then she said she doesn't feel the same after around 6-8
months of no contact. Did I wait too long?
She called me back but I didn't know what to say. Did I say
something wrong?
I said that I'd always be here if she needs someone. Would
she call me back again?
I think I've been hoping and overthinking too much. How
long has it been? 2 and a half years? Move on already and dry
those tears.

True

I wrote this for you
I hope it's not too late
I don't think of anyone but you
As my soulmate

You still don't realize
This look in my eyes
Is only for you
I'll always be true

For you I would do
Anything to move the
Sun and the stars if you asked
I would give you the moon and my heart

Gladly we were something
Extraordinary please
Don't tell me it's not you
Because I will always be true

Searching Soul

I'm struggling with a feeling
Like love isn't really something
I find like I've been dreaming
It isn't like that
It isn't like that
I wish I had a love to call my own
But I'm starting to think that in this cold world
There is no searching soul
To meet my tender loving arms and hold
On tightly
Great pretender, you don't change yourself to
Make her happier
That's not how it works
It isn't like that (no, no)
It isn't like that
Let me go
I don't wanna be in isolation but I don't want
To hold on to you if you'd rather be alone
So please say so
I love you, but if you leave I'll have to find a new beginning
I'll try a new path if it's just little ol' me wandering

Some of that Spice

Kiss everest with your lips
Eyes with closed lids
Hands cover face, fingers blink
Bedsheets loosely lying
The scent of artificial oranges
Prying petals from vigorous tulips
To taste like love without the
Seasoned heart's secret sauces
You thought you knew well enough
From just trying the free samples

Television

Is my heart gone
Or is it just me?
It sounds warm there and here
But it hurts to hear without the 't' in it
Trace back in slower rhymes
Tears fall in bottomless black terror
Travel and unravel back tact like no change
For vending machines
Then I re-read without any 't' in it
Service sales and false hopes, consumer
Where juices and jams pack fridges
Where appliances end and food begins
Make this life learn love and learn loss
Triple check to make sure that wishful idea is there
And plan to demand of yourself before you blame someone
else when it won't come true
Alas 24 hours ago is as gone as my heart
So it seems like simply me remaining
A bloodless pumpless lazy lump

Grocery Magics

Countertops, corner stores and antique shops
Your surfaces, a lemon zest vase
En passant, façade, croissant
You flaunt
Tailfeathers, professional nest tender
Don't surrender, pretender
Feelings caught in a blender
Brushstrokes paint your hair,
Your face in splendor
I want more but running out of canvas
Building blackboards back to basics
Brick by brick campus passes classes
In halls where mapless lovers cross paths
I gasp this time not because I held my breath
But because you took it away

I Am Joe's Heart
"I work hard to keep Joe alive. You know who I am. I am
Joe's Heart" - Lloyd Vernet Bridges Jr.

Haven't had an arrhythmia in a few months
Haven't an excuse to call those I am thinking about
A reminder to take a deep breath
Or even a good night's sleep
Maybe I'm crazy

I march to the beat of my own heart
When it rains I think about the ones I love
On the windowsill
Take a seat, make yourself at home
I don't talk, I just listen 'til I've heard it all

You probably don't remember
But you've been here before
You stand there, shouting in a tunnel
Was there someone on the other side?
Like I often do, I think it's time for me to let go
Because it's all in my mind
But even your emotions have an echo

The arrhythmia was back
As only but a murmur
A child of past decisions and heartaches
The music was only its opening act
And with it the memories came flooding back

You didn't know if you would fall at first
You didn't know any better
But you did

R Wave

~

The beauty in the fall is not in the word itself
But the helpless trust behind it
and getting up again after it hurts you

This unprompted allegro of a drumbeat
The body in shock
Some messed up physiological response to emotional
distress,
Or the body has a memory and it's experiencing post
traumatic stress
Either way, like clockwork, I feel the same sort of pain
Maybe I'm crazy

Brain Chemistry

Your brain is just chemical soup
They will tell you
After a heartbreak
Your love for someone becomes no more than an addiction
Your pain is simply withdrawal
They will tell you
The quantity of downsides should outweigh the magnitude of
the positive warm-and-fuzzy feelings
The quality of their company
And I'm not saying I disagree
For surely, I should be a man of science

My brain is an electrical putty
It melds and molds to the
Impressions of the last major influence
The latest scoop of cold truth
I bite into like a frosty treat
And then I brush my teeth with paste
Synaptically driven
My rusty volkswagen creaks and turns
Down streets and overthinks
Down memory lanes past
Rods and cones, retain my retinal
Rhodopsin before it stops at eye fields
Where the glossy panes peer
And drift down leaking channels through my mind's spheres

A Poem I Call "Chainsaw"

To do: Rage
What comes in must come back out
Like a chainsaw

Blade that cuts
That is not sharp deals all the more
Dull damage

Iron spills
Like the sap soaked attempt at defense
Of the trees

Breathe
Feel the exhaust you produce leave you
You're a machine

Clear a path
Nothing can stand in your way anymore
What fuels you?

A touch, a pull
Feeding into the cycle of your chains
You are in motion

You are petrified
Looking for someone to know deeply
But you only cut

Nostalgia

You are a chance encounter with a firefly
Wrapped warmly in light
Warped wings flapping like vibrating
Fiberglass sharp to the touch
I miss you so much

I am a fleeting dream or memory of a time
That I associate with a song
Don't get me wrong, I like the way all of it
Looks and sounds
I like the yellow flickers in the wet air, the pink fluff in the
walls, and just waking up in the morning wishing it lasted
longer, or that it was still fall
I'm getting a little tired of writing about my favorite things
that I miss
I can't remember the last time I saw a firefly
Or dreamt at all

One more kiss
Make me forget about all of this
I could never forget you, little miss
Cut to the chase to the same old place
We used to race past streetlights and sidewalk chalk
In your car I'd look at you
But forget about all that before it gets you down
Wait for a new love to be found
This life is like bound, bound, bound and
Rebound and
I think you can do it, if you give it a try

Author's Note

Dear reader,
Thank you for being here and supporting me and my first collection of poetry. This is a very special book to me. It peers into my own personal life experiences with love and loss. I really hope you enjoy it as much as I enjoyed finding myself while creating it. I look forward to writing my next works for you.

-   Love Joe